11.99

Science at the Edge

Internet Revolution

Ian Graham

Heinemann
LIBRARY

www.heinemann.co.uk/library
Visit our website to find out more information about **Heinemann Library** books.

To order:
☎ Phone 44 (0) 1865 888066
📄 Send a fax to 44 (0) 1865 314091
💻 Visit the Heinemann Bookshop at www.heinemann.co.uk/library to browse our catalogue and order online.

First published in Great Britain by Heinemann Library, Halley Court, Jordan Hill, Oxford OX2 8EJ, a division of Reed Educational and Professional Publishing Ltd. Heinemann is a registered trademark of Reed Educational and Professional Publishing Ltd.

OXFORD MELBOURNE AUCKLAND JOHANNESBURG BLANTYRE
GABORONE IBADAN PORTSMOUTH NH (USA) CHICAGO

© Reed Educational and Professional Publishing Ltd 2002
The moral right of the proprietor has been asserted.

Designed by Tinstar Design (www.tinstar.co.uk)
Illustrations by Art Constructions
Originated by Ambassador Litho Ltd.
Printed and bound by South China Printing Company Ltd. in Hong Kong/China

ISBN 0 431 14897 X
06 05 04 03 02
10 9 8 7 6 5 4 3 2 1

British Library Cataloguing in Publication Data
Graham, Ian 1953 –
　　　The Internet revolution. – (Science at the edge)
　　　1. Internet – Juvenile literature
　　　I.Title
　　　004.6'78

Acknowledgements
The Publishers would like to thank the following for permission to reproduce photographs:
Associated Press Photo Archive pp43, 53, 55, 56; b92.net p21; bankone.com p30; Corbis p34; Destinyschild.com p19; Madonnamusic.com p22; PA Photos pp7, 17, 38; Popperfoto pp6, 10, 11, 24, 25, 48, 49, 51; Reuters p50, Reuters/Mike Hutchings p4; Report Digital p54; Rex Features p14; Science Photo Library pp8, 15, 18, 20, 26, 28, 32, 36, 37, 41; Shout p40; Still Pictures/Jorgen Schytte p39; Thrust SSC/ Ian Graham p5

Cover photograph reproduced with permission of Science Photo Library.

Our thanks to David Hall for his assistance in the preparation of this book.

Every effort has been made to contact copyright holders of any material reproduced in this book. Any omissions will be rectified in subsequent printings if notice is given to the Publishers.

Disclaimer
All the Internet addresses (URLs) given in this book were valid at the time of going to press. However, due to the dynamic nature of the Internet, some addresses may have changed, or sites may have changed or ceased to exist since publication. While the author and Publishers regret any inconvenience this may cause readers, no responsibility for any such changes can be accepted by either the author or the Publishers.

Contents

Any words appearing in the text in bold, **like this**, are explained in the Glossary.

The Internet revolution

When Russian sailor Viktor Yazykov developed an abscess on his elbow, he guessed that it was serious. However, he couldn't just go to his doctor for treatment, because he was taking part in a solo round-the-world yacht race. He was on the first leg of the 1998 Around Alone race, from Charleston, South Carolina, to Cape Town, South Africa – more than 600 km away from the nearest port.

Do-It-Yourself surgery

His solution was to **e-mail** a doctor in the United States via his yacht's **satellite communications system**. Dr Daniel Carlin, a specialist in infectious diseases at the New England Medical Center in Massachusetts, knew the abscess could burst under the skin and trigger a fatal infection, so it had to be dealt with immediately. He gave Yazykov instructions by e-mail on how to cut into the abscess and drain it safely. With the surgery successfully completed, Yazykov faced a further problem. He had taken too much aspirin to cope with the pain of the surgery. One effect of aspirin is to thin the blood. As a result, his blood wouldn't clot and his wound wouldn't stop bleeding. Dr Carlin e-mailed him instructions to apply pressure to the wound to halt the bleeding. Without his satellite e-mail connection, Yazykov could have died. Dr Carlin started helping sailors, explorers and mountaineers in remote places by telephone and fax, but the introduction of the **Internet** in the mid-1990s has revolutionized his work. As well as being able to describe their injuries in text form, it enables patients to e-mail him **digital photographs** of their injuries. This gives him far more information than he could get from a description over the telephone or in a fax. When his medical centre receives an emergency e-mail, the system automatically activates staff pagers and mobile phones to summon help.

Round-the-world sailor Viktor Yazykov probably owes his life to medical advice he received by e-mail.

Fuel crisis!

As the Thrust SSC team prepared to go to the United States to set the first supersonic land speed record in 1997, they faced a problem. They had been loaned a heavy-lift transport plane to fly them there from Britain, but it came without fuel. They needed to buy a quarter of a million gallons of fuel for it. After spending millions of pounds developing and testing their jet-car, they risked losing the chance to set this unique record. Their American rival, Craig Breedlove, was also preparing to make the same record attempt in his own car.

They solved the problem by using their **website** to ask people to buy the fuel for them in US$25 (£18) lots. People all over the world were following the progress of the project on this website. When they saw the team's appeal for help, they started buying the fuel by typing their credit card numbers into the website. The fuel was paid for at the rate of up to 136,380 litres (30,000 gallons) a day.

As a result, Thrust SSC went to the USA and on 15 October 1997, the team set the first supersonic land speed record. Without the Internet, they could not have contacted so many people in so many places around the world for help and the record books might have told a different story!

Without the Internet sale of fuel certificates, the Thrust SSC team might not have been able to set the first supersonic land speed record.

Going online

It seems that today, if you want to be part of modern society, **Internet** access is almost essential. Internet users have a choice of more than eight million websites. About 500 million people had access to the Internet in mid-2001, almost double the 260 million who were **online** at the end of 1999. In China alone, the number of Internet users had exploded from 8.9 million in 1999 to 26.5 million in mid-2001.

Why the Internet?

The Internet was developed in the United States in the 1960s. At that time, a computer system consisted of one huge computer, called a mainframe, connected to lots of **terminals** with their own screens and keyboards. A mainframe was big enough to fill a room. Damaging the mainframe could knock out the whole computer system. ARPA (the Advanced Research Projects Agency) solved this problem by developing a new type of computer system, called a decentralized computer **network**. It had no central computer controlling everything, but was made from lots of smaller computers linked together in a network called **ARPAnet**. If one computer was damaged, the others still worked. If one link between them broke down, they could still send messages to each other by using different **links** – like finding a way round a traffic jam by using other roads. The network grew as more research agencies and universities joined it. In 1990, the US National Science Foundation took over control of ARPAnet and the other networks that, together, had become the Internet.

In the 1960s, a computer filled a whole room and needed a team of people to operate it.

Mobile access

In the beginning, using the Internet meant sitting at a computer at home or at work. The arrival of the Internet café let people 'surf the Net' in more public places. And now, people can go online using laptop or handheld computers or by means of mobile phones. **Mobile (wireless) Internet access** (see pages 10-11) is expected to be the most popular way of going online within a few years. The latest generation of mobile phones, called 3G (third generation), promises to offer faster access, faster downloads and better quality images than the older **WAP phones**.

An Internet bench enables people to go online outdoors by plugging their laptop computers into telephone sockets on the bench.

One of the strangest ways to go online is to plug into a park bench! In 2001, an Internet bench was set up in an English park. It allowed up to four people to connect to the Internet by plugging their laptops into the bench. However, this bench was vandalized shortly after it 'opened'. Elsewhere in England, a cyber-park enables up to twenty users at a time to use the Internet wirelessly, unlike the park bench. Wireless public access points, where you can access the Internet without having to plug your computer into something, are harder for vandals to damage.

Social contact

Some critics of the Internet paint a picture of people hunched over their computer screens, dangerously cut off from the real world. The reality is less clear. Some studies confirm that the hours that Internet users spend online might otherwise be spent doing other things, such as talking to friends and family. A survey carried out in the USA by psychologists at Stanford University, California, found that more hours online meant fewer hours in contact with 'real' people. However, another American survey found that 72 per cent of adults with an online account had visited a relative or friend the previous day, while only 61 per cent of those without an online account had done so. This survey also found that sending e-mails often led to follow-up contacts by telephone or in person.

The World Wide Web

In its early days, the Internet was so difficult to use that only academics bothered with it. The invention that transformed the Internet into the global phenomenon that millions use today was the World Wide Web.

The World Wide Web is an online library of millions of documents. Each document has its own unique address so that the network can find it. The documents are created by using a language called **hypertext mark-up language (html)**. A computer program called a **browser** enables computer users to request a Web document, **download** it and display it on a computer screen.

The World Wide Web made it so easy to find information online that millions of ordinary people connected to the Internet.

The birth of the Web

The Web was invented by Tim Berners-Lee and his team at the European Nuclear Research Centre (CERN) in 1990. It was released on the Internet for other people to use in 1991. Then in 1992, Marc Andreesen created the first user-friendly Web browser, called Mosaic. It was the first browser with links that could be clicked on to take the user to other pages. It was also the first browser to allow images and text to appear on the same page. By making the Internet easy to use, browsers like Mosaic and, later, Netscape and Internet Explorer, enabled millions of people to use the Web.

Net talk

The terms 'Internet' (or 'Net') and 'Web' are often used to mean the same thing, but they are not the same. The Internet can exist without the Web, but the Web cannot exist without the Internet. The Internet is a network of computers. The connections between these computers are the cables and radio links that carry their communications signals. The Web is a huge number of pages stored in Internet computers. The connections between the pages are the software links put there by the people who create the pages.

Glass cables

The Internet makes use of telephone networks. When long distance telegraph communication was invented in the nineteenth century, messages were carried by electric currents flowing along metal cables. Telephone calls were carried in the same way. In the 1950s, scientists discovered that light could carry information along thin strands of glass called optical fibres. In the 1970s, telephone companies began experimenting with sending telephone calls down optical fibres. The first optical fibre telephone line was laid in England in 1978. Now, optical cables link the world's major cities and carry much of the Internet's data. With the introduction of new broadband technology (see page 20), the amount of data that can be carried is greatly increasing. One hair-thin glass fibre can carry hundreds of thousands of voice and data calls at the same time.

Is it right to censor the Net?

The Web allows the free exchange of information and ideas – anyone can put his or her thoughts and opinions online. Some **websites** contain unpleasant material. Most are harmless, but some are a cause for concern – if they urge a person to commit a crime, for example. Parental controls, called censorware or nannyware, in browsers and programs can block access to some pages. Sometimes, censorware is also used to prevent access to websites dealing with lifestyles or politics that the agency providing the access disapproves of. Many people feel that this is censorship, not protection. Many websites contain objectionable material, but does that mean it is right to censor them? If so, who should decide what is acceptable?

'If computer science were a traditional science, [Tim] Berners-Lee would win a Nobel Prize.'

Eric Schmidt, Chief Executive Officer, Novell, talking about the inventor of the World Wide Web

The digital divide

While thirteen-year-old Myra Jodie was surfing the Web at her school in Arizona, USA, she found a website offering a computer as a prize. She typed in her details and won that computer. Arizona is the next state to California, where many of the world's leading computer and Internet companies are based. Even so, she couldn't use her new computer to surf the Web at home. Myra lived in a Navajo (a Native American tribe) reservation. In her neighbourhood, less than one home in four has a telephone – Myra's family did not have a telephone line, so she could not connect to the Internet. So, even in a wealthy country like the USA, there is a 'digital divide' between those who can access the Internet and all its benefits, and those who can't.

As few as 3 per cent of people in the poorest areas of a developed country may have access to the Internet, compared to more than 50 per cent of people in wealthier parts of the same country. One answer is to open **IT** (Information Technology) centres, where people can call in and go online, or to make the Internet available in public places, such as libraries. Another is to offer people free or cheap IT training courses. IT lessons at school also play an important part in introducing children to the Internet. Government schemes to supply second-hand computers to poorer families help, too.

Even in wealthy countries, there are some people who cannot afford access to the Internet. Increasingly they will form a new digital underclass.

Half the people in the world have never made a telephone call, never mind logged on to the Internet. Two billion people do not even have a reliable electricity supply to power a computer. As Internet use in developed countries grows, the developing world is being left behind, creating another digital divide. Africa is coming online, but the growth is mainly in large cities – most of the continent still has no Internet access. Even if it did, cost would prevent most people from going online. Internet access in Africa costs from approximately US$68 per month. This is about as much as someone in one of the continent's poorer countries earns in a year!

Mobile Internet access

The old-fashioned telephone system in some African countries is a major obstacle to introducing the Internet. In 1999, there were fewer telephone lines in the whole of Africa than in the central area of New York City in the USA, or in Tokyo, Japan. In the poorest African

countries, such as Mali, Niger and the Democratic Republic of the Congo, there are only about two telephone lines for every 1000 people. Continent-wide, only about 2 per cent of Africans have phones. Bringing that up to the global average of 10 per cent would cost US$60 billion. One answer is to use mobile telephones, although these are often considered to be less secure than traditional cable-based networks.

In developing countries in general, the use of mobile phones to access the Internet is growing twice as fast as in developed countries. There could be 729 million **mobile data subscribers** in developing countries by 2010, overtaking the numbers with standard phones. But again, this is confined mainly to major cities. Governments are beginning to recognize the problem and find ways to close the gap between rich and poor countries. Japan has pledged to provide US$15 billion over five years to help train IT experts in developing countries.

In Africa, where there are fewer land lines, the use of mobile phones for accessing data is growing faster than in developed countries.

Communication on the Internet

The **Internet** is mainly used to send e-mails. More than eight billion e-mails are sent every day. By 2005, that figure is expected to be 26 billion per day!

Getting the mail through

We can communicate with each other because the same words mean the same thing to different people (when you are talking the same language). In the same way, all computers connected to the Internet must process information in the same way or they wouldn't be able to make sense of it. The sets of rules about processing information used by computers that are connected to the Internet are called **protocols**.

The Internet's basic communication protocol is called TCP/IP. Among other things, this ensures that e-mails arrive safely. First, the TCP (Transmission Control Protocol) part splits information up into smaller **packets** of data. Then the IP (Internet Protocol) part labels them all with the address they are going to and sends them through the Internet.

Each packet of data travels on its own. Each Internet computer – called a **router** – that it passes through on the way reads its address and sends it on the next part of its journey by the fastest route. This means that the packets often travel by different routes and arrive in the wrong order. The TCP/IP software in the computer that receives them slots them back into the correct order. If any packets are lost, TCP/IP asks for them to be sent again. The information doesn't appear on the screen until all the packets have been received, checked and reassembled in the correct order.

A second important Internet protocol is File Transfer Protocol (FTP). FTP is a standard way of copying a file from one computer to another over the Internet. A file may contain data or it may be a computer program. Millions of files are stored on Internet computers – FTP enables Internet users to download these files onto their own computers.

Breaking down social barriers

You cannot tell someone's colour, age, religion, wealth or sex from an **e-mail**. This makes it difficult to discriminate against people. However, this can also be a problem, because you can't be sure that strangers who contact you are really who they claim to be. This can be dangerous, especially as most of the people who use Internet **chat rooms** and **IRC** are under twenty years old, and some are very much younger than that.

An e-mail is sent.

The e-mail is received.

An e-mail travels from computer to computer through the Internet until it reaches its destination. It is stored there until the person it is addressed to accesses it.

Another problem is that e-mails are easy to misunderstand. Most of the information we receive when we talk to people comes from the expressions on their faces, their body language, tone of voice and so on. E-mails contain none of this information, so it can be easy to give the wrong impression with a badly worded e-mail.

Younger people often use the same language in e-mails that they use in mobile phone text messages, for example, 'r u ok 2day?' In a recent survey, half of nine to twelve year olds said they expect e-mail to replace handwritten letters. Language experts feel that this may influence the way this generation uses language.

For more information about how to use chat rooms, IRC and e-mail safely, please see the first website listed on page 63.

Raising expectations

People who use e-mail often expect an instant response. If scores of e-mails arrive, all requiring an instant response, it can make normal work impossible. The average office worker already sends or receives about 40 e-mails every day.

Business communications

Companies use the Web to advertise the products and services they sell. They are happy to pay for equipment and training, because using the Internet can cut costs and improve customer service. This should in turn attract more customers, increase sales and lead to higher profits. E-mail is an efficient and cost-effective way for companies to communicate with their customers and suppliers. However, some companies use e-mail irresponsibly. They send the same promotional message to all the e-mail addresses they can get hold of. This is called 'spam' and it is the Internet equivalent of junk mail.

People often think that Internet communication means e-mailing text alone. In fact, the data that travels through the Internet can represent anything – including people's voices. Some people already use the Internet to make cheap or free telephone calls by using a microphone connected to their computer to send the call through the Internet. Companies could use the Internet for telephone calls, too, but they haven't because the quality of the sound is so unpredictable. When someone wants to speak to someone else via the Internet, that person's voice is **digitized** and divided into packets of **digital data**. The packets are then sent along communications channels chosen by Internet computers. Different packets will almost certainly travel along different **communications channels**. As some communications channels are better quality than others, the sound quality of a telephone call sent through the Internet can vary a lot. Poor sound quality means that companies will not use the public Internet for telephone calls.

Computer-satellite links mean information travels fast, even if the quality of digitized sound through Internet connections can be poor or suffer delays.

Voice Over Internet Protocol

Instead, they are beginning to use something different, called Voice Over Internet Protocol (**VOIP**), which does give them the guaranteed quality and reliability that they need. It also enables them to cut their communication costs. VOIP doesn't use the same public Internet **links** that the rest of us use. Instead, it uses tightly controlled communications links provided by a new type of communications company, called Internet Telephony Service Providers (ITSPs). These companies buy, rent or set up their own high-quality communications links and make them available to businesses for telephone calls and data communications.

What makes VOIP so useful is that voice and computer data can share the same communications channel at the same time and they are carried in the same form, using Internet Protocol. VOIP is particularly useful when people need to be able to talk to each other and also share data at the same time.

Internet Protocol (IP) Telephony

When a 'normal' telephone call is made, a circuit is set up to connect the two telephones. The circuit is used only for that one call. No one else can use it, even in the silences when no one is actually saying anything. This is very wasteful. It is more efficient to treat phone calls like Internet data. This is called Internet Protocol (IP) telephony. In this case, a caller's voice is changed into packets of data. Each packet is sent on its way separately in the next available free 'slot' in a communications channel – like fitting boxes into spaces on a busy conveyor belt. The same channel carries packets of data from many telephone calls. That way, lots of different calls can share the same channel at the same time, and costs are cut.

All types of businesses now depend on the Internet for accessing information and also for some of their communication needs.

Prioritization

Packets of data travelling through the public Internet are all treated in the same way. None of them is more important than any others. But packets travelling through business Internet channels are treated differently depending on what they represent. Voice packets are treated as being more important than the others. If packets of e-mail text or data are delayed or lost, all that happens is that information may take a little longer to appear on a screen. But if voice packets are delayed or lost, sound quality suffers. There may be gaps in the sound and, as a result, conversation may become difficult or impossible. Giving voice packets top priority eliminates this problem and guarantees good sound quality.

Virtual Private Networks

Large companies often have people working in several different places worldwide. Many of these companies are setting up their own Internet-style private **networks** to link their various offices together. These are known as Virtual Private Networks (VPNs), and they use VOIP to enable people to talk to each other and share data. For example, they might want to discuss a project while at the same time looking at designs or other information related to the project.

Some companies have decided not to use VOIP because they think Internet communications means poor quality and reliability. However, they are probably using it already without knowing it! Their telephone calls are probably travelling part of the way over Internet-style communications links called **IP backbones**.

Video over the Net

The TCP/IP rules (see page 12) that were developed to send e-mails were never actually intended to be used to send live sound or video pictures. If TCP/IP discovers that packets of data have been lost, it asks the sender to send the data again. That works well with e-mails and recorded sound and video clips. All the data is downloaded before the e-mail appears on the screen or the sound or video clip is played.

Live sound and video are different. They have to be played while the data is still being received. Your television set doesn't **download** a whole programme before showing it. It shows the pictures as soon as they are received. The Internet has to be able to handle sound and video in the same way. Internet companies have agreed on a set of rules for sending sound and pictures on the Internet. This is called **Real-time Transfer Protocol (RTP)**, because sound and video are called **real-time applications**.

Mobile phone and digital television companies have been testing RTP to make sure that they can all use it, too. RTP allows information to travel in one direction – from a broadcaster to an Internet user. Another protocol, called Real-Time **Streaming** Protocol (RTSP), allows two-way communication. Using it, viewers can, for example, rewind a movie or select a particular part of a video.

'Streaming is not television, yet, but it's a fundamentally more efficient way to deliver content over the Internet than other methods, such as downloading files.'

John Corcoran, Internet and digital new media stock analyst, CIBC World Markets

In future, most mobile phones will be able to receive colour video pictures and show them on the telephone's small screen.

The design revolution

Everything from paper clips and kitchen taps to cars and buildings have to be designed. The designs have to be approved by everyone involved in making and marketing them. As a result, designs have to go back and forth between various companies and individuals, sometimes in different countries. These designs are changed many times. Every change has to be approved by everyone involved and the revised drawings sent to everyone who needs them. Designs used to be printed on paper and sent by post or courier. They could take a week to make one journey. Now, designs are increasingly sent by e-mail, drastically cutting the time taken to approve them.

Creating designs on computers and sending them to everyone who needs to see them, by e-mail, speeds up projects.

Large construction projects can generate tens of thousands of drawings. All of them have to be distributed, checked, revised and approved. Distributing designs by e-mail has enabled such projects to be completed on time, within budget and with fewer errors due to misunderstandings over drawings. By the time the Heathrow Express rail link in England between central London and Heathrow Airport was completed in 1998, 24,000 drawings had been produced. Digital design, storage and distribution were used on the project from the beginning. The latest approved drawings could be received in the project office and forwarded to the construction site within minutes. As a result, the Heathrow Express was finished ahead of time and on budget – a rare achievement for such a complex project.

Digital design improves communication between designers or architects and their customers in another way. An architect can produce a **three-dimensional** computer drawing of a new building that enables a customer or a regulatory authority to see it from every angle. They can even 'walk' through it on the computer screen before a single brick is laid. This enables everyone to get a feel for what the building will look like and how it will fit into its surroundings. This means fewer changes have to be made after construction has begun.

Bypassing the media

All sorts of organizations, from the biggest charities to small clubs and societies, advertise themselves directly to the public through the Internet. The music and film industries also use the Internet to communicate directly with people. Fans of pop stars and movie stars traditionally learned about their idols through newspapers, magazines, radio and television. The Internet enables the stars, or the companies they work for, to provide fans with information, photographs, sound and video clips and merchandise by communicating directly with them through official **websites**. This also means that the stars and their companies get across information and news without a newspaper editor or television programme selecting the bits they want and editing them.

Official fan sites also provide recording and movie companies with valuable information about their customers and what they like. On the downside for the companies, unofficial websites can get undesirable stories to the public just as quickly.

Pop stars and rock bands communicate directly with fans all over the world through their official websites.

News and entertainment

It is now possible to hear radio programmes and see television programmes on the **Internet**. Broadcasters, including the BBC (British Broadcasting Corporation) and Radio India, make some of their programmes available **online**. Local radio stations all over the United States, Canada, Australia and some European countries put some of their programmes on the Internet, too. The demand, especially for live video, threatens to overtake the Internet's ability to supply it.

The broadband Internet

The Internet was designed for sending text. However, Web pages now contain a lot more than just text. There are graphics, animations (moving graphics),

photographs, sound clips and video pictures. All of these add to the amount of information that has to be transmitted. A **communications channel** is like a water pipe. The pipe can only carry a certain amount of water. In the same way, a communications channel cannot carry more information than it was designed for. This is its **bandwidth**. Moving pictures need more bandwidth than is available everywhere today. These 'big-bandwidth' services are described as **broadband**. The next generation of the Internet, the broadband Internet, is being introduced now to meet this demand. Progress is slower in some countries, such as Britain, Spain and China, than others, such as the United States, Germany, France and South Korea. About ten million US users had broadband Internet access in mid-2001.

Cables made from bundles of strands of glass carry Internet signals and telephone calls in the form of light beams.

News online

The Internet has had a surprising impact on news reporting. When broadcasters set up websites, they usually included **e-mail** access so that they could receive messages from their listeners and viewers. One unforeseen benefit of this is that it increases a broadcaster's news sources to include every listener and viewer with an Internet connection. As an important story breaks, some people who are caught up in it e-mail broadcasters with details.

The Internet war

In the 1990s, there was a war in the country that used to be called Yugoslavia, in eastern Europe. This war is described as the first Internet war. It was the first time that eyewitness reports from ordinary people caught up in a war appeared on the Internet. As aircraft bombed Serbia in 1999, hundreds of people who lived there e-mailed the BBC with accounts of the bombings. Thousands more sent messages to people all over the world and to Internet **chat rooms**. The value of these reports was that they were not edited or changed by the media. However, as they were not checked by anyone, no one could be sure that they were really true.

Picture perfect

Live video is now being put on websites. The pictures are taken by **web cameras**, or web cams. A web cam has no film. Instead, the pictures are taken electronically. Web cams can send live pictures of any place or any event to the rest of the world via the Internet. For example, web cams monitor the best surfing beaches around the world so that surfers can check on the size of waves rolling in. However, people are not always happy to have a web cam pointed at them. The owner of the Flat Iron Building in Chicago, USA, decided to place web cams in the building's hallways and put the residents' activities on the Internet. Perhaps understandably, the residents objected and the cameras had to be taken out.

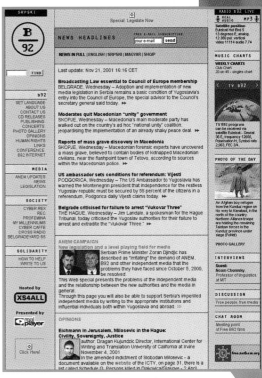

News websites, like this one run from Belgrade in Yugoslavia, often have details of an event available online within minutes of it happening anywhere in the world.

Webcasts

Some events, such as pop concerts, are shown live on the Internet. These 'Net-casts' are also called narrowcasts or webcasts. Distributing live audio and video on the Net is also called **streaming**, because the information is sent out in the form of a continuous stream of data. Live and recorded programmes and concerts are all now available for viewing as webcasts.

Pop goes the webcast

In 1999, the musician Paul McCartney played at the Cavern Club in Liverpool. Only 200 people were able to buy tickets to watch him in the tiny club. By webcasting the concert, millions of people were able to see it. In November 2000, Madonna's concert at the Brixton Academy in London was relayed via the Web. Nine million people logged on to watch.

Madonna's webcast of 6 songs over 29 minutes was watched by 9 million people over the Internet.

The trouble with webcasts

Webcasts seem to be a threat to 'normal' radio and television. However, they have severe shortcomings at the moment, and will not replace the experience of being present at a live event or watching it on a conventional television screen.

If you want to see a concert, you would not normally choose to watch it crouched over a tiny picture on your computer screen. The pictures are small and jerky, and it can be difficult to receive them at all if millions of other people are trying to log on to one **website** to see them at the same time.

Only those people who are lucky enough to have the fastest Internet connections can enjoy **DVD**-quality images. The much slower connections that most people have at home mean that image quality can be very poor.

For every person who managed to see Madonna's concert, there were many others who tried to access it without success. Connection problems can arise either because the website's own **servers** cannot cope with the numbers of people trying to log onto them, or because the **network** itself cannot carry the necessary volume of data. Faster Internet connections, greater bandwidth and higher capacity servers will be available in the next few years, and they should make it easier and more enjoyable to watch webcasts.

Caching technology

If too many people try to access the same Web page, Internet Service Providers (ISPs) sometimes try to ease the congestion by using 'caching technology'. They create a copy, or 'mirror', of a popular website on their own network. Users who access the website **download** pages from the ISP's mirror site, also called a cache site, not the original website.

If 1000 people try to access the same Web page, 1000 separate copies of the same page are sent back to them through the Internet. If their ISP sets up a cache site, the ISP downloads one copy of a page and passes it on to people who request it. As a result, caching dramatically reduces data **traffic** on the Internet.

Online music

Sound can be changed into digital form, copied perfectly and sent anywhere via the Internet. This is a major worry to the music industry! Sales of singles fell by 38 per cent in the US in 2000. The music industry blames this dramatic drop on the illegal distribution of music via the Internet, although many users of online music argue that sales were falling anyway.

Digital shoplifting

Every time a CD is sold, some of the money goes to the artist and some to the record company. Music downloaded free from the Internet deprives both the artists and the record companies of this money. Some artists, especially artists without recording contracts, are happy to make their music available on the Net free of charge. It gives them access to a worldwide audience, and someone might like their music and offer them a contract. There are websites that distribute and sell music legally, but music is also distributed and downloaded illegally on a huge scale. Artists and record companies see this as little more than theft – like stealing CDs from a shop without paying.

Sharing music

The music industry took music **piracy** more seriously with the arrival of Napster. This company made a computer program available that

Napster founder Shawn Fanning (left) and his lawyer, David Boise, make a statement to the press during the legal action against Napster's online music activities.

enabled anyone to find music files on other people's hard drives and download them on to their own computers. The RIAA (Recording Industry Association of America) took Napster to court to halt its activities. Napster responded by suspending its business while it changed its **software** to identify **copyright** music, which cannot be distributed legally in this way. It also did deals with some record companies so that it could legally sell their copyright music.

At the height of its success, more than 26 million people were using Napster. After the company was stopped from distributing copyright music, eight million people stopped using Napster and went elsewhere for their free music. Distribution of music via the Net is here to stay. Record companies themselves now recognize that the Internet is an important way to promote their artists and distribute music, so many of them are setting up their own online services.

MP3

Music is downloaded from the Internet in the form of MP3 files. MP3 stands for MPEG-1 layer 3 (MPEG is the Motion Picture Expert Group). It is a way of reducing the amount of information that has to be transmitted without noticeably losing any sound quality. As a result, the files take less time to download and they take up less storage space. A typical MP3 file compresses (squashes) a sound file to only one twelfth of its original size. In other words, a CD that normally holds about an hour of music could hold twelve hours of music in the form of MP3 files. MP3 files can be downloaded on to a computer or on to a small handheld MP3 player.

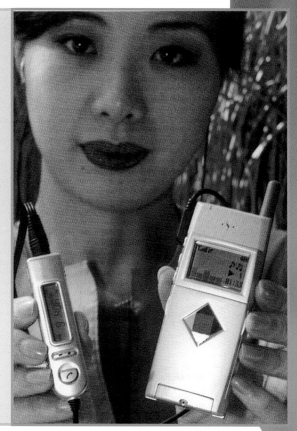

MP3 players, like these, store music downloaded from the World Wide Web. The stored music is listened to through earpieces or headphones.

E-commerce

Widespread buying and selling of goods on the **Internet** did not begin until 1994. Since then, an increasing number of companies have used the Internet as an important part of their marketing and trading. The Net enables them to reach customers all over the world. It also enables customers to shop from home and find the best prices. Doing business via the Internet is called electronic commerce, or e-commerce.

In the late 1990s, investors rushed to put money into new companies that sold products and services on the Internet, in the hope of making big profits. These Internet-based businesses became known as 'dot-com' companies, because their Web addresses often ended with '.com'. Some of the people who owned these dot-com businesses became millionaires overnight because so much money was invested in their companies. Unfortunately, many of these businesses failed because they could not attract enough customers. These failures discouraged many investors, and made it more difficult for new dot-com companies to raise money.

E-commerce makes it possible to buy goods online with only a few clicks of a mouse, but they still have to be stored, transported and delivered in the traditional way.

Changing shopping habits

Traditional shops risk losing customers as more people shop **online**. Already, 25 per cent of regular Internet users say they spend less time shopping in real shops. E-shopping has not grown as fast as it might though, because news of Internet crime makes many people reluctant to give their credit card details to companies on the Net. However, surveys indicate that shoppers' fears are declining.

Worldwide online sales of holidays alone reached almost £14 billion in 2000, an increase of 85 per cent over the previous year. The UK and Europe lag behind the United States in online shopping. In an online survey in 2000, only 3 per cent of British shoppers who took part said they shopped online regularly, while a similar US survey found that 48 per cent of respondents shopped online.

E-tailing concerns

Not all e-commerce growth is welcomed in all quarters. The Net is international, but most laws are only national. In the United States, even individual states can have different laws. The laws covering what may be sold vary from country to country and this causes problems when it comes to e-tailing (electronic retailing).

In France, it is illegal to sell or display anything that might encourage racism. When a **website** offered Nazi-related items for sale in 2000, a French judge ruled that the Internet Service Provider (ISP), Yahoo, had to make it impossible to access the site in France. Yahoo ensured that these items did not appear on its French service, but French Internet users could still see them by accessing Yahoo's US service. This case shows how difficult it is for ISPs to comply with all the laws in all the countries in the world.

Another worry for the authorities is the sale of medicines over the Net. Doctors worry that drugs bought via the Internet could pose a serious risk to patients trying to treat themselves. The US Food and Drug Administration has warned a dozen or more website operators that they could be committing a crime if they sell drugs to American citizens over the Internet.

> 'The question put before this court is whether a French jurisdiction can make a decision on the English content of an American site, run by an American company... for the sole reason that French users have access via the Internet.'
>
> Christophe Pecnard, Yahoo lawyer

Online publishing

One of the first industries to move to e-commerce was bookselling. Now, the texts of numerous books are available on the Internet. Some are books by unpublished authors seeking to bring their work to wider notice. Others are reproductions of books now out of copyright, such as those by William Shakespeare and Charles Dickens, which can be found on websites like Project Gutenburg (see page 63).

E-books

Publishers and authors are experimenting with publishing books on the Net. A book published in this way is called an electronic book, or e-book. E-books can be downloaded onto home computers or read on handheld devices no bigger than a paperback book.

If online publishing were to be popular with readers, it could change the way books are distributed and it could have serious implications for the bookselling trade. When the author Stephen King published a 66-page ghost story on the Net in 2000, 400,000 copies were ordered in one day – more than any of his best-sellers in print did on their first day in traditional bookshops. Some websites charged US$2.50 (£1.75) for it. Others gave it away free.

Stephen King returned to e-publishing in 2001, offering three snippets of his book *Dreamcatcher* as tasters for readers just before the book was published in the traditional way. The three 3000-word extracts were published online in the three weeks before the full-length book reached book shops.

Tomorrow's book? In future, you might download a classic or the latest best-seller onto your e-book instead of buying a conventional book from a book shop.

Best-sellers online

E-books might look like the future of publishing, but for the time being they have problems that will probably limit their popularity. There is always great demand for the latest Stephen King book, as there is for the latest offering from many best-selling authors. This in itself can cause problems. When Stephen King's ghost story was published, the Associated Press news agency attempted to access it for an astonishing 25 hours before they were able to download it. So many people were trying to use the same Internet servers at the same time that the system could not cope.

One serious disadvantage of the Internet when it comes to publishing is that the text of a book can be put on the Net and distributed without the publisher's permission. Pirate copies of books deprive authors and publishers of payment for their work, but it is almost impossible to stop it happening.

The future of publishing

Will e-books replace traditional print books? Probably not. Congestion on the Internet caused by thousands of people all trying to download the same best-seller at the same time is frustrating. Even when that problem is solved, many people will still prefer the experience of turning the pages of a printed book. Printed books are also very robust. They don't break down if they are dropped on the ground or a drink is spilled on them. They don't require any knowledge of how to use technology in order to read them. They don't need batteries. On the other hand, children growing up now, in a world of palm computers and mobile data phones, may prefer e-books to printed text on paper.

The future of publishing probably does not lie in an 'either-or' choice between traditional books and e-books. A new technology rarely completely replaces an existing popular technology. The two will probably exist side-by-side, like CD and tape, TV and radio, cinema and TV, and electronic games and board games.

'We see a time in the not too distant future when virtually every book in print will be available in both physical and electronic formats.'
Steve Riggio, vice chairman of US bookseller barnesandnoble.com

Financial services

It is now possible to buy insurance, take out a loan, apply for a credit card or open a bank account on the Internet. These online services usually cost less or offer better interest rates than the same services over a bank counter. Online banking lets customers run their bank accounts without having to go to banks during the few hours in the day when they are open. Online banks are open seven days a week, 24 hours a day, and are accessible from the user's home and, increasingly, by mobile phone, too. They also provide banking services to less populated areas – for example, to more remote parts of Australia.

By the end of 2000, about 20 million Europeans were banking online, roughly double the number of Americans using online banking at the same time. A market report published in mid-2001 predicted that e-banking in Europe would triple by 2005. And as online services available via mobile phones develop, up to 150 million people worldwide could be using wireless online banking by then.

PERSONAL FINANCE

SMALL BUSINESS

COMMERCIAL

PRIVATE CLIENT SERVICES

CORPORATE INVESTMENTS

BANK ONLINE

INVEST ONLINE

Online banking gives customers 24-hour access to their accounts. Bills can be paid and statements viewed by the customer at any time.

Fears over security

The growth of online banking has, however, been held back by customers' worries about security. Many people say they are worried about the security of their personal details on the Net. Internet banks have been hit by **hackers**. At least four British Internet banks are reported to have lost several hundred thousand pounds each as a result of hacker attacks. Furthermore, banks rarely announce that they have been attacked in this way, in case it shakes public confidence in them even more.

Profits first?

Banks are keen to go online, because it enables them to make higher profits. Each transaction, such as paying a bill, carried out on the Internet costs just one tenth as much as the same transaction carried out in a bricks-and-mortar bank. Making payments by telephone, interactive television or online instead of by cheque means that banks can process billions fewer cheques every year. However, banking online also means that far fewer people go into banks, so bank branches have been closed and staff numbers cut. During the 1990s in Britain alone, almost 4000 bank branches were closed and 200,000 banking jobs were lost.

Branch closures, even on this scale, do not make much difference to large towns and cities, but some villages and small towns have lost their only bank. Older residents and the less affluent are particularly badly hit by local bank closures. They are the least likely to be able to use Internet banking.

Sorry, you're the wrong sort of customer!

The Internet enables banks to collect more information about their customers, the services they use and how much profit they make for the bank. With this information, banks are likely to be less willing to take on customers who won't make them any money – for example, people who do not take out loans or use any services that the bank can charge for. In future, it could become more difficult to open a bank account if you are not the sort of customer the bank is looking for.

Business-to-business

There are lots of companies that don't sell their products and services to the public. Instead, they do business with other companies. This is called business-to-business commerce, or **B2B**. By trading electronically on the Internet instead of by post, phone and fax, businesses can trade with each other faster and more efficiently. As every communication, decision and action carried out electronically is automatically recorded, this gives companies a wealth of information about their activities. Analysing this information can help to show companies what needs to be done to improve their businesses.

Virtual market places

Once businesses begin to trade with each other electronically, they can set up a virtual market place on the Internet. A virtual market place is a website where companies that work in the same industry can buy and sell their products and services. The steel, car-making and

Construction is one of the industries that now uses the virtual market place to bring suppliers and customers together online to do business.

aerospace industries all have their own virtual market places. Architecture, engineering and construction (AEC) companies, mainly in the United States, use virtual market places, too. A virtual market place enables, for example, a construction business to invite companies to supply building materials, to agree prices and then exchange contracts digitally. All of this business-to-business negotiation used to be done by a chaotic mixture of telephone calls, faxes and letters.

Business-to-business commerce may seem rather boring, but it is very important, because it is worth about ten times as much as electronic trading with the public. It was worth $US400 (£275) billion in 2000, and is expected to grow to up to $US7 (£4.8) trillion by 2004. Electronic trading in virtual market places can save companies a lot of money. In one of the biggest business-to-business industry market-place projects, British Airways cut its number of UK suppliers from 14,000 to 2000 and saved more than £210 million.

> 'If you make savings in your basic business process, that has a quick impact on the bottom line (profit).'
>> David Oates, European vice president of Moai, a company that produces **software** used in electronic market places

Brutal new world

Business activities happen faster than ever before because of electronic trading and communication. Companies that trade with each other often work together very closely. It is important for them to choose the right partner companies. Electronic trading and virtual market places enable companies to set up connections between each other quickly. If they don't work, their electronic connections can be cut quickly, too. Businesses used to work at the speed of letter-post and telephone calls, but now they work at the speed of a mouse-click.

Fair competition?

Some governments and regulatory authorities are worried about the effect of virtual market places on competition. In many countries, it is illegal for rival companies to fix the prices of their products instead of competing with each other. Groups of companies that do this are called **cartels**. Competition drives prices down, but cartels keep them high. The European Union Competition Commission and the US Federal Trade Commission are watching virtual market places and their effect on competition and prices very closely.

The way we work

The **Internet** is changing the way we work. Some of the changes are improvements, but others are causing concern. For people who work mainly with ideas, knowledge and information, work need no longer be done only in a central office. By using the Internet, people can work at home. By using portable computers, people can access the Internet from anywhere. They can work out of the office, while visiting customers, abroad and even on a beach or while sitting in a park. For the first time, some people can work anywhere while also staying in touch with their colleagues and employers.

When they are away from the office they can access their company's files **online** and communicate by **e-mail**. This cuts the amount of time wasted when information used

Mobile Internet access enables people to work anywhere, but it also makes it more difficult to get away from work for a break.

to be unavailable, when communication was impossible or while staff were travelling. It also means that fewer journeys have to be made, saving companies both time and money.

Working in teams

Companies have traditionally been based on departments. In a manufacturing company, one department designs products. Another department buys in all the parts and materials needed to make them. Another markets the finished products. Other departments deal with the company's personnel (workers), its money and looking after its buildings. Departments are not, however, always the best way to work on a project.

The Internet could enable companies to work differently. They could set up teams of the best people for each project. By using the Internet a team could include people from outside the company. The Internet would **link** them all together as if they were working in one office. Everyone in the team would be able to see exactly what stage the project was at, from anywhere, 24 hours a day. They could track every new development as soon as it happened. As a result, there would be no confusion over which team member had the latest information, where files were located or whether important tasks had been done.

Of course, not all work involving the Internet is office based. Collaborative working over distance using the Internet is also being done in other areas, such as music. Musicians working in different locations can each take different channels on a song (with one playing the drums, another playing guitar, and so on) which is then put together in a central location.

Creating workaholics

The Internet enables people to work better, faster and smarter. This should lead to people getting all their work done in less time, or getting more work done in the same time. However, research shows that in an increasingly competitive business world, it actually results in many people working even longer hours. The Internet gives workers 24-hour access to company information and services, so work no longer has to stop just because the office has closed for the day. Some employees continue to work when they get home in the evening or even when they are supposed to be on holiday! Indeed, in a survey of more than 4000 US adults, only one in 25 said the Net had enabled them to cut their working hours.

Private Internets

The Internet is such a good way of distributing information that large companies are now using it for this purpose. However, they are not using the public Internet. They are setting up their own private Internet-style **networks** called intranets. An intranet stores and transmits information from computer to computer within a company in the same way as the Internet does. This means that information in a company's intranet can be sent anywhere in the world, by the Internet if necessary, because it is already stored in the right form.

The UK **telecommunications** giant BT (British Telecom) was one of the first companies to set up an intranet. In 1994, it had more than 100,000 employees in 38 countries, including the United States. It cost the company up to £20 million to print and mail a large document to every member of its sales force in all of those countries. By using intranet technology instead of mailings to keep them up to date, BT saved an astonishing £747 million in 1997.

A spy in the office

Using the Internet, intranet and e-mail lets employers monitor their workers' activities more closely than ever before. A survey carried out in 2001 suggests that companies have good reason to watch

their employees. Nearly half of office workers questioned admitted spending more than three hours a week **surfing** the Net while they were at work (although some studies say this actually makes them more productive, not less).

Some people say that monitoring workers like this is a sinister way of spying on them. It might be used to collect evidence to get rid of employees a company does not like. Other people say it is a way for companies to protect themselves against improper use of the Internet and e-mail at work. And, they say, it can actually benefit some workers by proving that they have not been misusing the Internet.

This change in working methods not only brings dramatic cost savings, it also changes the way people work. Employees cannot say that they have not been sent information they need, because it is all available on the company's intranet. This gives workers more control over their work and also more responsibility for it. It becomes their responsibility to collect all the information they need instead of waiting for the company to supply it. Having seen the power of the intranet to transform their own company, BT joined forces with Microsoft and MCI Communications to supply intranet systems to other companies.

The chance to work

People who are physically disabled often find it more difficult to get a job than able-bodied people. The Internet makes it harder for employers to discriminate against disabled people. It can make it possible for disabled people to compete for work more fairly with everyone else. At a time when increasing numbers of employees are working from home by using computers and the Internet, the fact that someone is, for example, confined to a wheelchair should not make any difference to his or her ability to work.

Computers and the Internet can help people with disabilities compete on more equal terms with the able-bodied.

Shrinking the world

By enabling people to communicate and work together so easily, wherever they are, the Internet has the effect of shrinking the world. If everyone within an organization, and outside it, communicates by e-mail or through a virtual market place, a worker's location becomes less important. It does not matter whether they are in the same building or in a different country. This means that it is not important to live in cities any more, or to travel between a home in the country and a city work place – the Internet makes it possible to work or to run a business equally well from a small village.

The Internet also enables companies to hire at least some of their workers from a far wider area than was possible just a few years ago. For example, an American computer systems company could hire **software** writers in Ireland. An electronics company in Australia could use designers in Germany. A French transport company could use architects in Sweden. International co-operation between businesses is not a new thing. But today, thanks to the Internet, it is easier than ever.

Employers and workers do not need to be located in the same place any more because they can be linked together via the Internet. This journalist can use the Internet via his satellite telephone system to send reports and photographs from Nepal.

Cutting labour costs

The Internet gives skilled workers a much wider choice of employers. It also makes it easier for companies to hire workers in countries where labour costs are the lowest. If it is less expensive to hire computer programmers in India, for example, compared to programmers in Switzerland or Finland, then the Indian programmers will get the work. That is great if you are an Indian programmer, but not so good if you are a programmer living in a high-wage European country, Australia or North America.

But workers in low-wage countries are beginning to realize their worth on the world market. In 2001, freelance computer programmers in Russia earned about US$10 (£7) per hour. By advertising on the Internet, an enterprising Russian programmer could find work with companies in other countries, including the United States and Canada, at US$50 (£35) per hour – five times the local rate.

Other workers will be increasingly reluctant to accept less payment for the same work than workers receive in other countries. Disputes about differences in pay are common between workers within the same company, city or country. The Internet is transforming these local disputes into international issues.

Rates of pay

What is the correct payment for a piece of work? Is it what someone in California earns? Or is it what someone in Moscow, Calcutta or Beijing earns? And if someone, for example, living in Delhi is employed by a company in, say, San Francisco, how should they be paid – according to the rate for the job in the United States, or the rate for the job in India? By realizing their value and raising their pay rates to the same as those in high-wage countries, workers could eliminate the very reason that employers seek them out and hire them.

Workers in developing countries can sell their technical skills to employers anywhere in the world thanks to the Internet.

Big Brother is watching you

Personal privacy on the **Internet** is a very important issue. A survey carried out at North Carolina State University, USA, found that people tend to go **online** more if they know their activities and **e-mails** are not being watched or looked at.

Most people know that it is a bad idea to give personal details to anyone who should not have them, but the Internet enables other people to collect information about you without your knowledge or permission. Some **websites** use data files called **cookies**, which contain information about the people who visit. Some of these cookies are then stored on your computer's hard drive and used to keep track of return visits to the same sites and to build up profiles of visitors. They can also be used to personalize websites for regular visitors. Your computer might have thousands of cookies stored on it, each one giving information about you to someone else without your knowledge every time you go online. The European Union has considered banning cookies, but the companies who use them say it would damage the quality of their service to customers.

Police forces use the Internet to trace criminals and their online activities. Some police forces have specialist 'cyber teams' to tackle Internet crime.

Making cookies

When you visit a website, it automatically makes a list of the pages you look at. This file of information is a cookie. Unless you change your **browser** settings, the cookie is sent to your computer and stored on its hard disk. The next time you visit the same website, it searches your computer for its cookie. It may use the information in it to choose which advertisements or special offers to show you. It then updates the cookie with the new pages you have looked at and stores it on your hard disk again.

Making use of cookies

Information in cookies could reveal something that a person would prefer to keep private, such as his or her political interests. Cookies identify a particular computer, and that computer is usually in the user's home. It is theoretically possible to combine data from cookies with information from elsewhere to find out who users are and where they live. Most cookies are read only by the websites that created them, so the information should be confidential. However, there is nothing to stop companies from sharing cookie data.

When data passes through an Internet computer, the computer makes a record of where the data has come from and where it goes. This information is used to monitor the amount of **traffic** on the Internet and how it changes from minute to minute. It is possible to use this information to track people's activities on the Net. However, it is so difficult to link the information to individual computer users, that it is normally only used by law enforcement agencies to trace criminals.

The ways people use the Internet, the websites they visit and the pages they look at are of great interest to advertisers and marketing companies selling goods and services.

Websites also record which of their pages and **links** are clicked on. This is called 'clickstream information'. Companies that place advertisements on websites are keen to use it to study which advertisements are the most popular.

> 'People disclose four times as much information by e-mail as they do face to face.'
>
> Adam Joinson, psychologist, Open University, UK

To scramble or not to scramble?

One of the hottest issues facing Internet users and lawmakers at the moment is encryption. Encryption means scrambling information before sending it through the Internet so that it cannot be read by anyone who intercepts it.

Uncrackable codes

Sending an e-mail is like sending a postcard. Although it is not easy for an unauthorized person to intercept an e-mail, it is certainly possible to do so. Few of us worry, because most of our e-mails would mean very little to anyone else. We rely on the sheer volume of e-mail to hide our own messages. However, there are many people who need to be sure that an unauthorized person cannot read information. Companies may want to send e-mails containing confidential commercial information, or information about employees' pay or personal details. Doctors may want to send messages that include the details of a patient's medical history. If they **encrypt** the information, they can hide it from unauthorized spying.

Widely available encryption programs 'scramble' the information, so that anyone who intercepts it sees meaningless gobbledegook. Encryption is already used to scramble the credit card details of customers buying goods on the Internet. The process is not more widely used because people do not see any need for it! The trouble with encryption is that it works too well. The best mathematical codes used for encryption today are almost uncrackable. Even the police cannot unscramble e-mails encrypted using them. Law enforcement agencies worry that encryption will let criminals communicate with each other without any chance of their messages being traced and decoded.

One key or two?

Messages are encrypted using a number called a **key** to turn the message into gibberish. The bigger the number, the more difficult it is to decrypt, or 'crack', the code and read the message. Encryption based on a 40-digit or 56-digit key can be cracked. Encryption based on a 128-digit key is 4700 million million million times more difficult to crack. There are encryption systems that use a 1024-digit key. The developers of a 2048-key encryption system estimate that it would take 30 billion years to crack!

The simplest encryption system uses the same key to encrypt and decrypt a message. The weakness of this is that the key has to be sent from the sender to the receiver. Anyone who finds it or steals it can unscramble the message. A safer method uses two keys, one public and one secret. A message is encrypted using the recipient's public key, which is available for anyone to use. It can only be decrypted using the recipient's secret key. The secret key does not have to be sent to anyone, so there is less chance of it being stolen.

The US Embassy in Nairobi in Kenya lies in ruins after it was bombed by terrorists in 1998. Governments are concerned about the use of encrypted e-mails in planning attacks like this.

Spying on surfers

Governments also monitor how much their citizens use the Internet. The more repressive governments are not the only ones that do it. In 2001, Members of the European Parliament (MEPs) warned Internet users to encrypt their e-mails, or they could be read by a UK-US spy **network** called Echelon. Neither government has admitted Echelon's existence, but the MEPs are certain that it exists and that it is being used to intercept private communications.

A question of control

Some governments would like to be able to control encryption. They and their law enforcement agencies want to be able to decrypt, or unscramble, e-mails at will. Failing that, they would like to make the use of encryption by the general public illegal. The Chinese government introduced regulations forcing people to hand over encryption codes used in their computers and mobile phones. Objections from international businesses persuaded the government to relax the regulations for e-mails, mobile phones and computer operating systems.

'If I don't want it broadcast in public, then I don't do it on the Net.'
Susan Landau, Sun Microsystems

Security

As soon as computers are linked together, **hackers** can attack them. Hackers use the **Internet** to break into computer systems. They may do more than just look at the information. They may steal or change it, or even put the computer system out of action. Organizations protect their computer systems in a number of ways. **Passwords** stop most people, but these can be guessed or stolen. Another security measure is the **firewall**, a program that checks all incoming traffic to make sure it is authorized.

Denial of service

One of the most troublesome hacker attacks is the **denial of service** attack. It makes a **website** unusable without actually cracking its security or breaking into it. A hacker floods the website with so much **traffic** that the communications system is overwhelmed, denying access to genuine users.

A **distributed denial of service** attack is even more difficult to deal with. This is when attack programs are planted in 'innocent' computers around the world. The programs lie dormant, doing nothing until a pre-arranged time. At the appointed time, all the computers contact

The Millennium Bug

The operation and security of the Internet was threatened at the end of 1999 because of the way computers were programmed. When computers were introduced, memory was so expensive and in such short supply that none was wasted. Dates were stored with just two digits for the year. So, 1995 was stored as '95'. At one minute past midnight on 1 January 2000, computers would set the year to '00', but they would not know if it was 1900 or 2000. There were fears that computerized systems could fail. It was called the Y2K (meaning 'Year 2000') problem, or the Millennium Bug. Thousands of computers were checked and reprogrammed. In the event, there were only a few minor problems. In Australia, a bus ticket checking system failed. In Italy, telephone bills were dated 1900!

the same website again and again, overloading it with traffic. Distributed denial of service attacks rely on the fact that many computers linked to the Internet have poor security, allowing hackers to plant attack programs in them. When an attack begins, the targeted website can do little about it. Well-known organizations like Yahoo, Amazon and CNN were hit by a series of denial of service attacks in February 2000.

'When businesses say they are not being "hacked", they are not telling the truth.'

Bill Hughes, Director-General of the UK National Crime Squad

Computer security

Computer systems are often protected by using programs called firewalls. They monitor the **e-mail** flowing in and out, and block anything that might cause a problem. They work like security guards checking people entering and leaving a building. One type of firewall checks where data has come from and where it is going. It is programmed to reject anything coming from or going to certain addresses. Another type of firewall reads the data as well as its address.

This is slower but more secure. Some parts of an organization's computer network may be open to the public via the Internet. Other parts may be accessible only by the organization's own staff. Yet others may contain the most sensitive data, available to a very small number of people within the organization. To achieve this, there may be a series of firewalls, each providing a higher level of security than the one before.

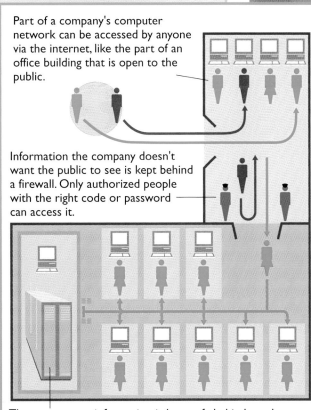

Part of a company's computer network can be accessed by anyone via the internet, like the part of an office building that is open to the public.

Information the company doesn't want the public to see is kept behind a firewall. Only authorized people with the right code or password can access it.

The most secret information is kept safe behind another, more secure, firewall.

Catching a virus

Damaging programs called viruses can spread from computer to computer around the world through the Internet. American businesses lose US$550 (£380) million a year due to **virus** attacks. Early viruses infected only the one computer that unwittingly downloaded them. But now, viruses often use the electronic address book stored in a computer's e-mail program to mail themselves automatically to more computers.

The Melissa virus was unleashed in March 1999. It automatically e-mailed itself to the first 50 contacts in each computer's address book. It took a few days to spread round the world. In May 2000, a more damaging virus, the Love Bug, swept through Asia, Europe and finally the United States, within a few hours. It arrived on people's systems as a message entitled ILOVEYOU. Many people who received it automatically opened it. Unfortunately, doing this activated the virus. The virus e-mailed itself to every contact in the computer's address book and also destroyed any photographs and music files.

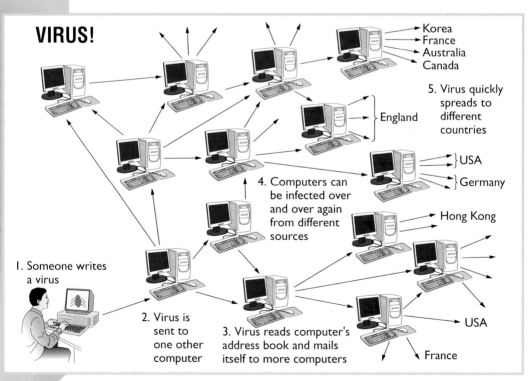

VIRUS!

Korea
France
Australia
Canada

5. Virus quickly spreads to different countries

England

USA
Germany

4. Computers can be infected over and over again from different sources

Hong Kong

1. Someone writes a virus

USA

2. Virus is sent to one other computer

3. Virus reads computer's address book and mails itself to more computers

France

Computer viruses spread from computer to computer around the world by e-mailing themselves to other Internet users. It is possible to protect your computer by installing anti-virus software. However, this software is only as good as its latest update, as new viruses are appearing all the the time.

Military viruses

Military forces rely on computerized command, control and communication systems. Some countries are therefore researching the use of computer viruses as weapons. In 2000, the head of Taiwan's Defence Ministry's Information and Communications Bureau announced that Taiwan had about 1000 computer viruses. It would use them to repel an electronic attack from its neighbour and long-time enemy, China.

Other countries and also terrorist groups are fast realizing that cyber attacks can bring an enemy to its knees just as effectively as traditional weapons of war, such as guns and bombs. In addition to the same **network** jamming and denial of service attacks that hackers use, military forces have developed 'Trojan horse viruses'. These lie undetected inside enemy computer systems. There, they trace passwords that open top-secret parts of their military command and communications networks. There are also fast-breeding 'worm viruses' that infect a system and then copy themselves over and over again so quickly that they scramble entire computer networks. There are even said to be video viruses that create images to mislead enemies.

The United States is thought to be the world leader in developing **cyber weapons**. The US Defence Department is said to have a US$1.4 billion budget solely for cyber warfare. A few terrorist groups and government agencies are thought to have used cyber weapons in a very limited way. However, no one knows precisely what would happen in a widespread cyber attack, and exactly how much damage military viruses might do.

Inventing viruses

The term 'computer virus' was coined in 1983 by US computer security expert Fred Cohen to describe computer programs that can insert copies of themselves into other programs – just like a biological virus infecting living cells. Three years earlier, **ARPAnet**, the forerunner of the Internet, had been brought to a halt by the accidental release of a virus, probably the first in history. In 1988, a virus written by Robert Morris, a student at Cornell University, brought most of the early Internet system to a halt. When the arrival of the Web attracted millions more people to the Internet, the numbers of viruses rocketed. About 200 new viruses are identified every month.

Cyber crime

Internet crime, or **cyber crime**, is rising at an alarming rate. In a survey of American companies and government agencies in 2001, 64 per cent reported that they had suffered financial losses due to breaches in computer security in the previous year. In most cases, the criminals attacked through the organization's connection to the Internet. Cyber crime is such a serious problem that police forces have had to set up specialist cyber teams to deal with it.

A US FBI agent goes to work. Thousands of 'cyber crimes' are reported to the FBI every year. In February 1998 the FBI set up a special department to deal with threats to national security posed by cyber crime.

Long-distance theft

Most cyber crime is not committed by hi-tech criminals breaking into computer systems. The Internet enables criminals to commit traditional crimes of theft, such as fraud (tricking people out of money), over much longer distances and to find many more victims. They might create a website offering get-rich-quick schemes or investments with impossibly high returns to trick people into investing money with them.

Piracy

Software **piracy** is a growing international crime. Software of all sorts – computer programs, games, music and films – is stolen, copied and distributed illegally via the Internet. About 270,000 copies of Hollywood films are downloaded illegally from the Internet every day, and the figure is rising rapidly. The computer software industry estimates that it loses more than US$10 (£7) billion a year due to piracy. In the USA, about 25 per cent of the computer software sold is pirated. In some parts of the world, mainly South-East Asia and eastern Europe, up to 95 per cent of all computer software sold is pirated.

> 'You'll see just about every program that's popular being offered and downloaded on the Internet.'
>
> Bob Kruger, vice president of enforcement for the Business Software Alliance

Insider trading – cyber-style

In the major stock exchanges of the world, like the New York Stock Exchange shown right, **insider trading** has become a problem. A few people have been found guilty of insider trading on the Net. Someone who has shares in a company creates a website that appears to be giving reliable and impartial news about the financial markets and company performance. A news story on this website announces a forthcoming merger or take-over that will boost the company's value. As a result, people start investing in the company by buying shares. The value of the company, and therefore its share price, rises. The person behind the website then sells his or her shares for more than was paid for them and makes a profit. Credit card fraud is common, too. Criminals steal credit card numbers, clone cards (make copies of real cards) or use **software** that creates false card numbers. Once they have a credit card number, they can use it to obtain goods, services or cash.

Cyber police

If financial crime on the Internet, particularly fraud and piracy, is not controlled, it will slow down the growth of e-commerce. People will be reluctant to do business over the Internet and, in particular, to trust their credit card details to Internet companies. The American financial regulator, the Securities and Exchange Commission, employs a cyber crime force of more than 200 lawyers, accountants and investigators to look for Internet fraud. It has now set up a computer system that automatically searches through Internet sites and looks for criminal activities, which the cyber force can act against.

In 2000, the United States' authorities organized a worldwide operation called 'Get-rich-quick-dot-con' to identify fraudulent websites. Police and consumer organizations in 28 countries took part. They found more than 1600 websites that appeared to be breaking the law.

Politics and the Net

Some governments are not just wary of the **Internet**; they see it as a serious threat to their power to govern their own populations.

People in countries dominated by repressive regimes, or regimes that distrust western news media, use the Internet to access news and information about what is happening in the rest of the world. This information may not be easily available in their own country. In countries where computer ownership is rare or where there are few telephone lines, Internet cafés have sprung up to satisfy the demand for Internet access. In China alone, 60,000 Internet cafés were opened.

In July 2001, the Chinese government closed 2000 of these cafés and ordered another 6000 to suspend Internet activities. The government claimed to be responding to genuine concerns from parents about the damaging influence of the Internet on their children. Parents were said to be alarmed at the way their children seemed to be addicted to the Net. However, the government took measures to monitor and limit Internet access that went beyond protecting children.

In many countries, people surf the Net in Internet cafés. Some governments are so suspicious of the Internet that they have closed the cafés or restricted their activities.

It blocked access to **websites** run by dissidents (political opponents) and some foreign media. It is also reported to be forcing Internet cafés to install **software** that will automatically alert the police if certain sites are accessed. The government licenses local providers of news on the Net, and the use of foreign news in their content is banned.

China is not alone in trying to restrict and control access to the Internet within its borders. Burma, Vietnam, North Korea, Malaysia and some Middle Eastern countries have all taken steps to censor Internet content, limit access or record the identities of people using the Internet. In some places, Burma for example, even owning computer equipment that is capable of connecting to the Internet can result in a lengthy prison sentence.

Information and misinformation

In democratic countries (countries where the people elect their own governments), people are beginning to use the Internet to get more information about candidates standing for election and their policies. The Internet can provide more information than they can obtain from the carefully managed and scripted appearances of politicians in the media. In the 2000 Bush-Gore presidential election in the USA, both George W. Bush and Al Gore had their own websites, which were regularly updated with the latest news and events about their campaigns. Organizations that supported the two candidates also put up websites, campaigning for each man's election. Their opponents also used the Internet to point out their shortcomings. Some websites went further. **Misinformation** about candidates can be spread so quickly via the Internet that it can severely damage a candidate's election prospects. Political parties have to watch the Web very carefully and be ready to deal with any incorrect information that appears.

US presidential candidates George W. Bush and Al Gore kept voters informed about their policies and campaigns via their websites during the 2000 election.

Clumsy legislation

Governments deal with problems by passing new laws. There is a danger that some laws intended to deal with **cyber crime** could stifle freedom of speech on the Internet. A report by the US-based Internet Council recommends that governments should educate Net users in how to protect themselves and their personal information when **online**. It also calls on governments to deal with the potential weaknesses and dangers of the Internet to users internationally rather than nationally. But inevitably, politicians and courts in different countries make their own independent decisions about the Internet and what appears on it.

Some people would like to 'clean up' the Internet by forcing Internet Service Providers (ISPs) to be legally responsible for every website, **chat room** and **e-mail** on their networks. Every Web page, chat room message and e-mail would have to be checked before it appeared on an Internet user's screen. For example, saying something that damages someone's reputation is called defamation, and it is a crime. Internet Service Providers would have to ensure that everything passing through their **network** contained nothing that might break this or any other law. At a time when everyone wants faster access, it would slow **traffic** on the Internet to a snail's pace. It would also sharply increase the cost of Internet services at a time when service providers are being urged to cut prices. And finally, it would lead to thousands of websites and millions of e-mails being rejected because they might risk the ISP being prosecuted. In short, it would cripple the Internet overnight.

Some treat ISPs as publishers, who are responsible for everything that appears on their networks. Others treat ISPs in the same way as telephone companies, who are not responsible for the messages carried on their networks. This leaves ISPs in a difficult position.

'The public would not be well served by compelling (ISPs) to examine and screen millions of e-mail communications, on pain of liability for defamation.'

US Appeals Court ruling

'Governments need to recognize the amazing benefits of the Internet and do nothing to cripple it.'

US Internet Council

Direct action

Governments have not welcomed the way the Internet enables political activists to organize themselves nationally and internationally, and to arrange protests at important political meetings. People are free to protest in a democratic society. However, the Internet enables political activists to organize demonstrations on a scale that risks interfering with democratic government. The dates and venues of political meeting and events are posted on websites run by protest groups.

When government heads met in Genoa, Italy, in 2001, 10,000 demonstrators from 700 protest groups descended on the city to make their views known. The cost of policing these sprawling demonstrations, which can attract violent individuals and groups, is enormous.

The Internet enables protest groups to organize demonstrations, but the numbers of people they attract can make these gatherings difficult to police.

Online voting

The numbers of people who vote in elections are falling dramatically all over the world. The United States, Britain, Europe, some African countries and the Far East are all experiencing this problem. Everyone agrees that this is bad for democracy. Some countries, such as Australia, have dealt with it by making voting compulsory. Around 95 per cent of people there vote, but since they have been forced to vote, do they really care about who gets their vote or who wins an election?

Others think the decline in voting could be halted by introducing online voting. Younger people in particular would like to have the opportunity to vote online. Surveys show that less than 40 per cent of teenagers and people in their twenties vote today, but more than 70 per cent of them said they would vote online if they could. Instead of having to go to a voting booth during its opening hours, online voting could be available round the clock from anywhere. Everyone could vote from home or work using PCs or from **terminals** in shopping centres and malls.

Voting in the traditional way involves the use of ballot papers that have to be counted by hand or sometimes by machine.

Paper and punch card problems

Most states in the USA are investigating online voting systems. The first online vote has already taken place within the Democratic Party in Arizona. Online voting could involve people more in local and national politics and encourage more of them to vote. It could also eliminate situations like the problems during the 2000 US presidential election, when officials in Florida spent weeks trying to figure out what voters' intentions were.

People voted by punching a hole in the ballot paper next to their chosen candidate. This type of voting paper can be checked and counted by machine. Some voters had punched the holes in the wrong way. There were also technical problems with the machinery. Punch-card voting systems have an error rate of 2 to 5 per cent. As long as the result of an election is not closer than this, the error rate does not matter.

Weighing up the issues

Paper and punched card voting have their problems, but online voting is not perfect either. The question is, do the advantages outweigh the disadvantages? The Net could make it so easy to vote that politicians, pressure groups and local authorities could turn to online voting to settle all sorts of issues. However, the effect of holding a lot more polls could be to turn people off voting even more than now. Also, while younger voters would welcome the chance to vote online, some older voters, who have not grown up with the Internet, might distrust it so much that they would be less likely to vote.

The cost of online voting

The cost of converting to online voting is beyond many authorities. One county in California, USA, spent US$14 (£9.6) million setting up an electronic voting system. Few local authorities in the United States or elsewhere can afford this sort of expense. Security and privacy are major considerations too, especially if the system is to let people vote using their home PCs. Few home computers are secure, and election websites could be attacked by **hackers**, so online voting could be a security nightmare. As a result, the US National Science Foundation has embarked on a study to investigate online voting.

The decline in the numbers of people taking part in elections may be halted by introducing electronic voting via the Internet or through digital television.

Conclusion

The ways in which the **Internet** affects our lives changes almost daily. It is therefore very difficult to give a 'snapshot' view of the state of the technology and how it is being used that is not instantly out of date. Anyone who wants to live without the Internet can do so now, but in many countries it will soon become as difficult to avoid as telephones and television. It certainly looks as if the Internet is fast becoming one of those technologies that are not so much 'must have' as 'cannot do without'. Of course, there are also many people for whom the Internet is an expensive luxury that they cannot afford.

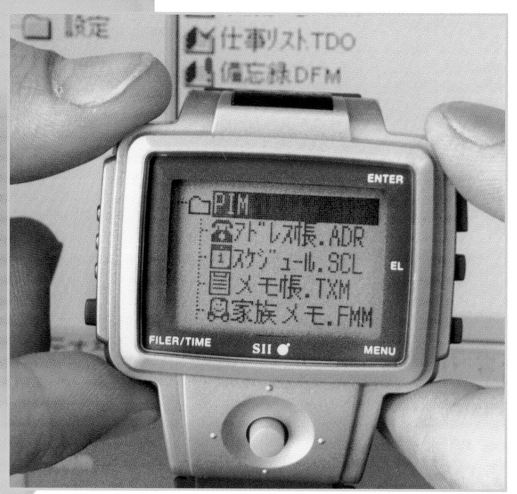

Instead of carrying portable computers or mobile phones for going **online**, in future we may wear Internet devices, such as the recently developed Internet watch.

Internet evolution

Despite its rapid growth, enormous popularity in the home and great value to business, the Internet today is still at an early stage of development. Cheaper computers that can provide faster Internet access will increase Internet usage and make new high-speed services possible. Many of them will be portable and wireless. And the development of universal standards for exchanging data means that most new services should be accessible by a variety of different devices, including mobile phones, PCs and digital televisions. **Mobile Internet access** means that **surfing** the Web and communicating by **e-mail** will no longer be something that can only be done sat down at a computer on a desk. It will increasingly be something that we have with us wherever we go, like wearing a watch. The implication of this is that the Internet is bound to become a bigger part of all our lives.

Leaping into a New World

The development of all countries to date has always begun with a mainly agricultural society and economy. Then, the country goes through an industrial revolution, mirroring the original industrial revolutions that transformed Western economies in the nineteenth century. From there, it moves into a modern, post-industrial economy. The Internet can help developing countries to leap straight from a mainly agricultural economy to a post-industrial economy without having to go through the heavy industrial manufacturing stage. It can do this by enabling people in developing countries to offer services to the global market place. This used to happen only after a country had established a history of international trade in manufactured goods.

However, the Internet is a form of communications technology that records everything we look at, everything we buy and every message we write. This raises privacy issues that we should all be concerned about. The way some governments continue to try to control the Internet or restrict people's access to it is worrying. And the ease with which criminals are able to use the Internet to further their criminal intentions is a cause for concern, too. Some people think the Internet is as important an invention as electricity or the car and that it will transform our society as much as those inventions did. Others think it will destroy personal privacy and social values. No one knows which of these is correct... yet.

'Don't get too attached to current technologies. One thing is certain – everything is about to change.'

US Internet pioneer Dr Vinton Cerf

Timeline

1969 **ARPAnet**, the forerunner of the **Internet**, is established.
The first computer-to computer link-up is made between computers at the University of California Los Angeles (UCLA) and the Stanford Research Institute, both in the USA.

1971 The first **e-mail** program is written by computer engineer Ray Tomlinson.

1980 A **virus** is accidentally released onto ARPAnet, bringing the **network** to a halt.

1983 ARPAnet is divided into separate military and civilian services.
US computer security expert Fred Cohen invents the term 'computer virus'.

1986 Evidence of **hacker** activity is discovered at the University of California Berkeley.
An investigation results in the arrest of five German hackers.

1989 Tim Berners-Lee and Robert Cailliau begin the work that will lead to the World Wide Web.

1990 The US National Science Foundation takes over control of ARPAnet and the other networks that had become the Internet.

1992 The World Wide Web is opened to public access.
Marc Andreesen creates the first user-friendly Web **browser**, called Mosaic.

1993 Three million people are using the Internet.
US Vice President Al Gore popularizes the term 'information superhighway' for the World Wide Web.

1994 Hackers break into the US bank Citibank's computers and steal more than US$10 (£7) million from customers' accounts. All but US$400,000 (£246,000) of the money is eventually recovered.

1995 Computer user Christopher Pile becomes the first person in the United Kingdom to be imprisoned for writing and releasing a computer virus. Hackers attack US Defense Department computers 250,000 times.

1997 1.5 million **websites** are **online**.
4000 cases of Internet fraud are reported to the FBI in the United States.
The computer manufacturer, Dell, announces online sales of US$10 million per day.

1998 130 million people are using the Internet.
2.8 million websites are online.
40,000 **cyber crimes** are reported to the police in Britain.
8000 cases of Internet fraud are reported to the FBI in the United States.
Viktor Yazykov performs surgery on his arm during a round-the-world yacht race by following instructions sent to him by e-mail.

1999 Europe's biggest **software piracy** operation, worth US$237 (£160) million, is shut down after advertisements for pirated software seen on the Internet are traced to a gang based in Denmark.
260 million people are using the Internet.
4.8 million websites are online.
Computer programmer David Smith is arrested for writing and releasing the Melissa virus. It infects millions of computers worldwide and causes more than US$80 (£56) million of damage.
At the end of the year, the Pentagon closes many US military websites in case weaknesses caused by the Millennium Bug give hackers an easy way into government and military computers. In the event, the Millennium Bug causes few problems.

2000 7.4 million websites are online.
Internet Service Provider AOL merges with media giant Time Warner. This gives AOL's Internet services access to Time Warner's television programmes, news services, films and recorded music.
The ILOVEYOU virus infects computers worldwide.
The world's first online election takes place within the Democratic Party in Arizona, USA.
Best-selling author Stephen King publishes his story 'Riding the Bullet' on the Web.

2001 500 million people are using the Internet.
8.7 million websites are online.
Ten million people have **broadband** access to the Internet in the USA.

Glossary

ARPAnet Advanced Research Projects Agency network. ARPA net is the US computer network that developed into the Internet.

B2B business-to-business. Trading between companies instead of between companies and the public.

bandwidth amount of information a communications channel can carry every second. A narrow bandwidth channel can carry text. Live video has to move much more information per second, so it needs more bandwidth. Large bandwidth is also called broadband.

broadband see bandwidth

browsers computer program used for viewing Web pages

cartels rival companies who agree on the prices of their products instead of competing against each other by cutting prices. Cartels keep prices high.

chat rooms pages on the Web where several people can 'chat' to each other by typing messages on their computer keyboards. Whatever they type appears on the Web page for everyone to see.

communications channel pathway shared by lots of different messages. It may be a metal cable, a fibre-optic cable, a radio signal or a combination of these.

cookies short files of information created by a website. They are stored in an Internet user's computer so that the website can recognize repeat visitors.

copyright right to publish, copy or sell printed, artistic or musical work. None of these can be done legally without the permission of the copyright owner.

cyber crime crime committed by using the Internet

cyber weapons computer programs, such as viruses, used to attack an enemy's computer systems

denial of service attack on a website that stops other people from using it by flooding it with so many requests for data that its servers are overwhelmed.

digital data data (information) in the form of digits (numbers)

digital photographs photographs taken by a digital camera, in the form of a series of numbers so that they can be stored in a computer

digitized changed into digital form (a series of numbers)

distributed denial of service denial of service attack on a website made from many different computers in different places simultaneously

download copy a program or data from a large to a small computer. Sending programs or data in the opposite direction is called uploading.

DVD Digital Versatile Disc. A type of computer disk similar to a CD that can hold different forms of information, including computer programs, data, music and films.

e-mail electronic mail. Messages (mainly text) in digital form sent from one computer to another through a network such as the Internet.

encrypt to hide information or a message by using a secret code to stop unauthorized people from reading it

firewall computer program that stops unauthorized people from accessing a computer system

hackers someone who gains unauthorized access to a computer system, especially via the Internet

HDTV High-Definition Television. A television broadcasting system with very high quality pictures.

hypertext mark-up language (html) the computer language used to create Web pages

insider trading using inside information to influence the stock market

Internet global network of inter-linked computer networks

IP backbones the main pathways for information travelling through the Internet

IRC Internet Relay Chat. IRC enables people to communicate by typing text messages. The messages appear on the screens of all the computers connected to the same virtual meeting place, called a channel.

IT Information Technology. The use of communications systems and computers for the storage, processing and distribution of information.

key number used to decrypt, or decode, an encrypted message, like using a door key to open a lock

links connections. Web links, or hyperlinks, are the clickable areas on Web pages that automatically download new Web pages.

misinformation wrong information

mobile data subscribers people who receive Internet data by using mobile phones

mobile (wireless) Internet access a way of receiving information from the Internet by radio instead of using a cable or telephone line

MP3 standard way of compressing audio files to make them smaller, so that it is easier, quicker and less expensive to send them through the Internet

network collection of interconnected pieces of equipment, such as computers or telephones

online connected to the Internet

packets units of data that contain the data itself plus the address it came from and the address it is going to

passwords secret words that work like keys to let people use computer systems or look at information stored in computers. The system works, or the information appears, only if the correct password is keyed into the computer.

piracy illegal production, use or sale of information that is protected by copyright

protocol set of rules that describes a standard way for networks or the equipment connected to them to exchange data

real-time applications computer programs that process information and display the results as soon as the information arrives, instead of waiting for all that information to arrive before displaying the results

Real-time Transfer Protocol (RTP) set of rules for information to be distributed via the Internet and played in real time instead of waiting for the whole file to be downloaded before playing it

router computer that receives Internet or intranet data and passes it on to the next computer on its way to its destination

satellite communications system system for sending messages over long distances by using satellites in space

servers computers that make services available on a network. Internet servers receive requests for Web pages and send the pages back.

software computer programs, the instructions that make a computer work

streaming distributing live sound and video pictures on the Web

surfing moving from page to page around the Web

telecommunications communicating over long distances by using electricity, radio waves or light

terminals devices with screens and keyboards used to enter information into a computer and display the computer's output

three-dimensional having thickness in all three directions (length, breadth and depth), like objects in the real world

traffic all the messages that travel through a communications channel or a whole network, such as the Internet

virus unwanted computer program that spreads itself from computer to computer through a network. Some viruses damage files in the computers they infect.

VOIP Voice Over Internet Protocol. A standard way to send voices through the Internet or an intranet.

WAP (Wireless Application Protocol) phones mobile phones that can connect to the Internet, download limited information from the Web and send and receive e-mails

web cameras (web cams) digital cameras that produce pictures viewed on the World Wide Web

website collection of related Web pages

Sources of information

Further reading

The Internet, Lisa Hughes, Hodder Children's Books, 1998
The Internet Made Simple, P. K. McBride, Butterworth Heinemann, 2000
The Internet: The Rough Guide, Angus J. Kennedy, Rough Guides Ltd, 2001
Thrust, Richard Noble, Transworld Publishers, 1998
The Timetables of Technology, edited by Bunch and Hellemans,
   Touchstone/Simon & Schuster, 1994

Websites

http://www.wiseuptothenet.co.uk A UK government website containing lots of information about how to use the Internet safely.

http://news.bbc.co.uk The home page of BBC News, with an extensive, searchable database of articles on all subjects, including the Internet.

http://www.newsweek.com The website of *Newsweek* magazine, with a searchable database of articles on all subjects, including the Internet.

http://promo.net/pg/ The Project Gutenberg website, containing hundreds of out-of-copyright books that can be downloaded for free.

http://www.quackwatch.com A website that warns against incorrect and damaging health and medical advice given on the Internet.

http://whatis.techtarget.com Definitions and explanations of a wide range of technology words, including those related to the Internet.

http://www.fbi.gov Website of the US Federal Bureau of Investigation, the US law enforcement agency that deals with Internet crimes. It includes a link to a children's area (http://www.fbi.gov/kids/6th12th/6th12th.htm).

http://newconnections.gov.au This is the website of the Australian department of Communications, Information Technology and the Arts. It covers new Internet developments in Australia.

Index

Titles in the *Science at the Edge* series include:

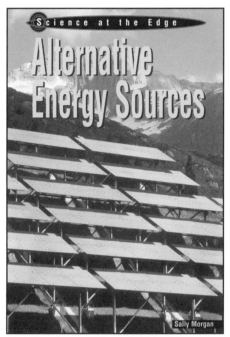

Hardback   0 431 14895 3

Hardback   0 431 14894 5

Hardback   0 431 14896 1

Hardback   0 431 14897 X

Find out about the other titles in this series on our website www.heinemann.co.uk/library